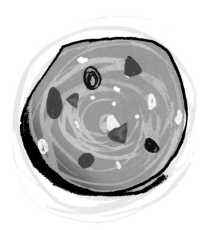

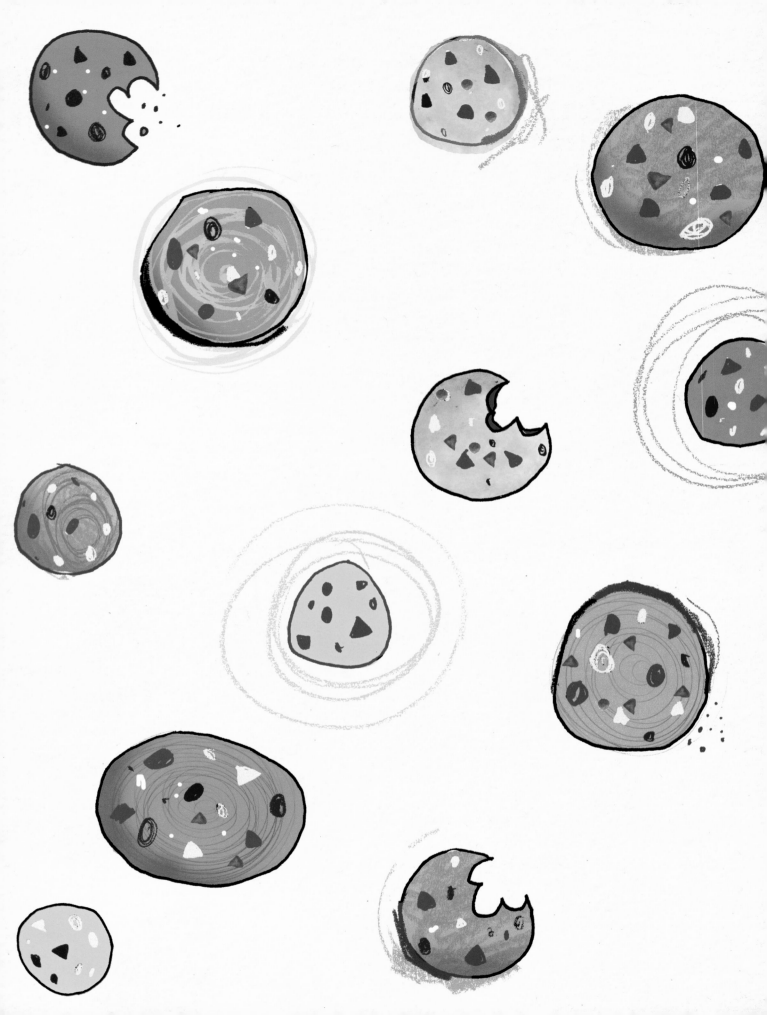

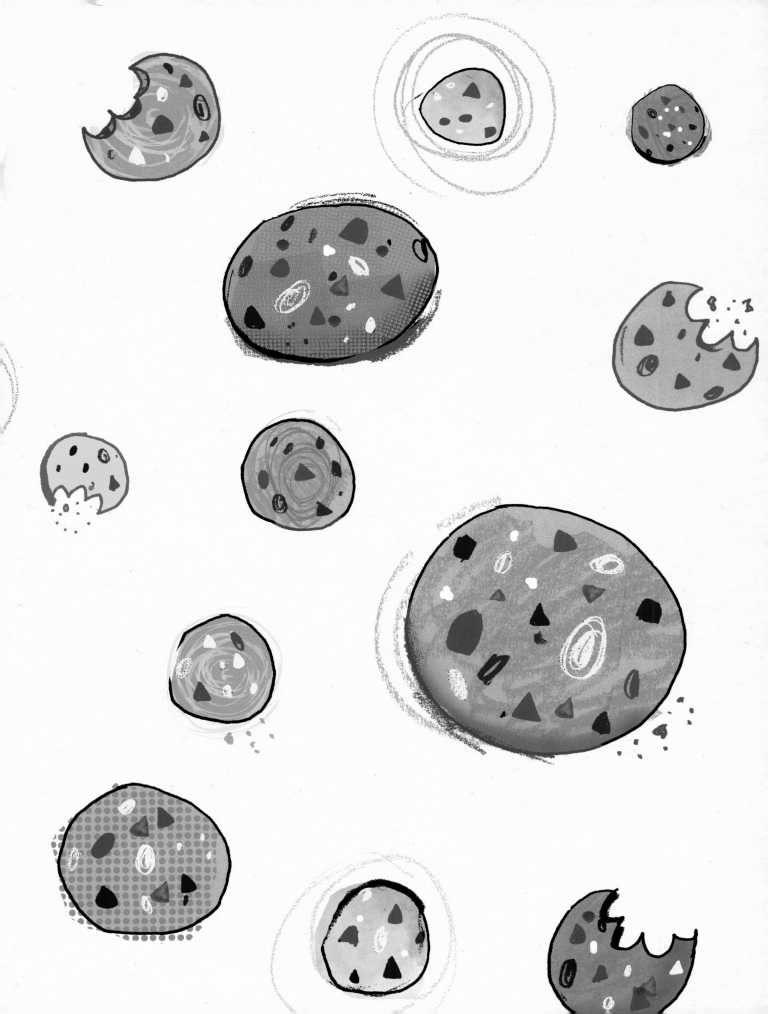

In memory of my mum — J.R.

For Dan x — C.E.

First published in Great Britain in 2014
This edition published 2015
Deepdene Lodge, Deepdene Avenue,
Dorking, Surrey, RH5 4AT, UK
www.bonnierpublishing.com

Text © Jamie Rix, 2014
Illustrations copyright © Clare Elsom, 2014

Printed and bound in China

ISBN: 978 1 84812 493 6 (paperback)

1 3 5 7 9 10 8 6 4 2

The Last Chocolate Chip Cookie

Jamie Rix

Illustrated by Clare Elsom

Piccadilly

There was one chocolate chip cookie left on the plate, so I leaned across the table and took it.

"Jack," gasped my mum.
"Where are your manners? Offer the
last chocolate chip cookie to
everyone else first."

"EVERYONE else?" I said.
"EVERYONE else," she insisted.

So I put the last chocolate chip cookie
in my pocket and did as I was told.

I offered it
to my brother,
but he didn't want it.

I offered it to my dad, but he didn't want it.

I offered it to Gran,

and even to the cat,

but they didn't want it.

So I offered the last chocolate chip cookie to my teacher,

the window cleaner,

the bus driver,

I went all round the world and offered
it to anyone I could find, including
a Mexican marzipan-maker with a moustache.

But no one wanted it.

So I took the last chocolate chip cookie
into space and offered
it to an alien.

But the alien didn't want to eat the last chocolate chip cookie . . .

He wanted to eat ME!

"Splagly!" gasped his alien mumma.
"Where are your manners?
Offer the human being to everyone else first."

"EVERYONE else?" he said.

"EVERYONE else," she insisted.

So Splagly put me in his pocket and did as he was told.

He offered me to his brotter, his daddle, his grin-gran,

the cattamog, his tin teacher, the window wiper,

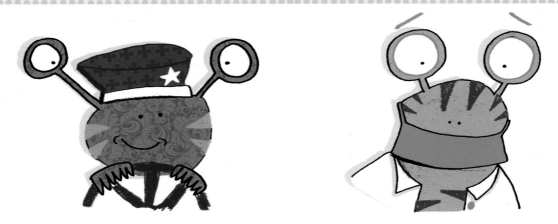

the spacebus pilot and the fang-filler.

He flew all round the universe and offered me
to any alien he could find . . .
including a four-eyed
Bogly Marsh-masher.

But no one wanted me . . .

. . . until he arrived back on Earth

and offered me to my mum.

"Yes, I would like him, please," she said.

"It's lovely to meet an alien with such good manners."

I told my mum that I'd offered the last chocolate chip cookie to everyone else but no one had wanted it.

"Then you can eat it," she said.
"It will taste twice as delicious now
that you've been so polite."

As I took it out of my pocket I was drooling.

I'd waited a long time to eat the last chocolate chip cookie.

I took a bite . . .

IT TASTED LIKE

CARBOARD

GUNK-GLOOP

WITH HAIRS

ON IT!

DO YOU want the last chocolate chip cookie?

LAST CHOCOLATE CHIP COOKIE RECIPE:

YOU NEED:

- 175g butter
- 225g caster sugar
- 2x eggs
- 350g x self raising flour
- 100g x chocolate chips

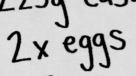

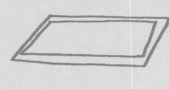

GET COOKING: *

Pre-heat oven to 180°

Add all ingredients to bowl and mix well

Spoon dollops of the mixture onto baking tray

(grease the tray first and leave lots of room between each one)

Bake in oven for 15-20 minutes until golden

EAT AND ENJOY AND DON'T LEAVE THEM IN YOUR POCKET TILL THEY'RE MOULDY!

* get an adult to help with the oven!

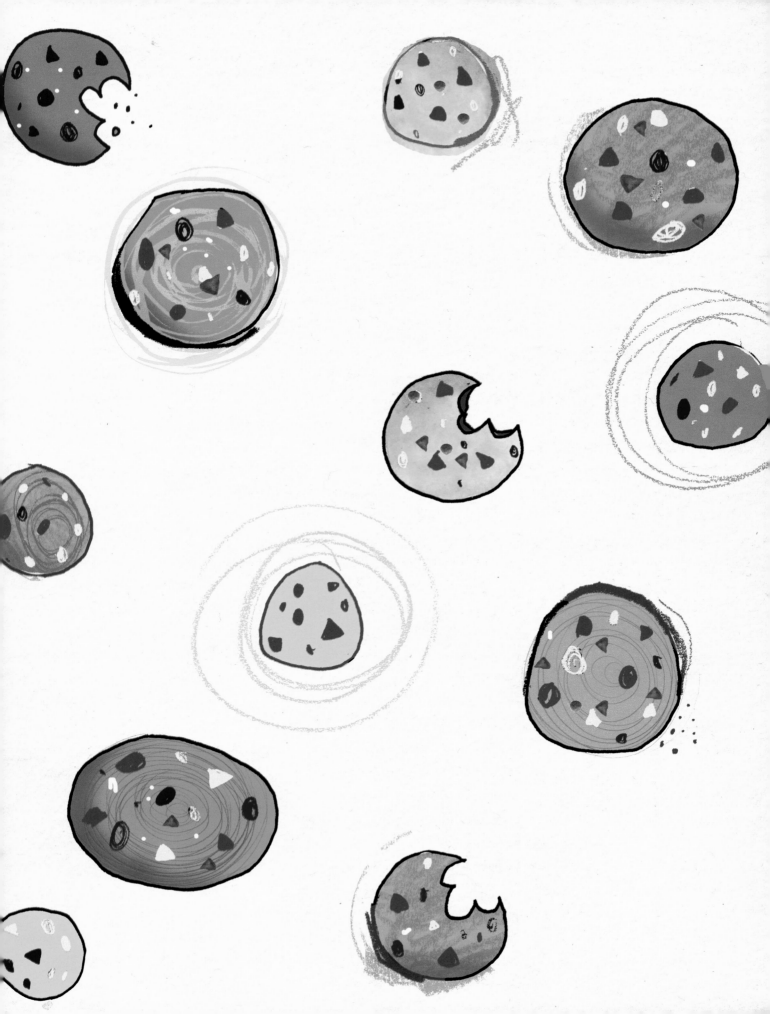